LET'S-READ-AND-FIND-OUT SCIENCE®

STAGE 2

Terrible Tyrannosaurs

BY Kathleen Weidner Zoehfeld

ILLUSTRATED BY Lucia Washburn

HarperCollins Publishers

For Robert and Geoffrey
—K.W.Z.

For Jeffrey, Jamie, Andrew, and Daniel
—L.W.

Special thanks to Dr. John R. Horner,
Curator of the Museum of the Rockies at Montana State University,
for his time and expert review

The *Let's-Read-and-Find-Out Science* book series was originated by Dr. Franklyn M. Branley, Astronomer Emeritus and former Chairman of the American Museum—Hayden Planetarium, and was formerly co-edited by him and Dr. Roma Gans, Professor Emeritus of Childhood Education, Teachers College, Columbia University. Text and illustrations for each of the books in the series are checked for accuracy by an expert in the relevant field. For more information about Let's-Read-and-Find-Out Science books, write to HarperCollins Children's Books, 1350 Avenue of the Americas, New York, NY 10019, or visit our web site at www.letsreadandfindout.com.

Library of Congress Cataloging-in-Publication Data
Zoehfeld, Kathleen Weidner.
  Terrible tyrannosaurs / by Kathleen Weidner Zoehfeld ; illustrated by Lucia Washburn.
    p.   cm. — (Let's-read-and-find-out)
  Summary: Describes what fossils tell us about the physical characteristics and behavior of the large carnivorous Tyrannosaurus rex.
    ISBN 0-06-027933-8. — ISBN 0-06-027934-6 (lib. bdg.)
    ISBN 0-06-445181-X (pbk.)
    1. Tyrannosaurus rex—Juvenile literature.   [1. Tyrannosaurus rex.   2. Dinosaurs.   3. Fossils.   4. Paleontology.]
  I. Washburn, Lucia, ill.   II. Title.   III. Series.
QE862.S3Z64   2001   99-32925
567.912'9—dc21   CIP
                                                                                            AC

Typography by Elynn Cohen
❖
1 2 3 4 5 6 7 8 9 10
First Edition

Terrible Tyrannosaurs

The most terrifying thing about a *Tyrannosaurus rex* is its teeth. Or maybe it's the fact that all those teeth—as many as fifty to sixty—grew in jaws that could open wide enough to swallow a grown person in one gulp.

Luckily, we don't have to worry about a *Tyrannosaurus rex* swallowing us. The last *T. rex* died more than 65 million years ago, along with all the other dinosaurs that lived then. We know *T. rex* only from its bones.

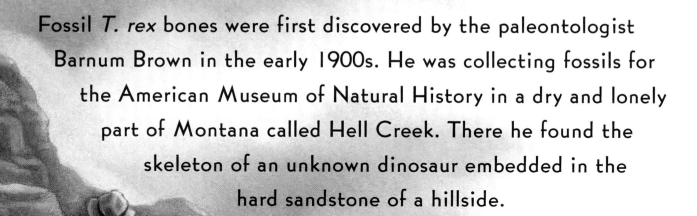

Fossil *T. rex* bones were first discovered by the paleontologist Barnum Brown in the early 1900s. He was collecting fossils for the American Museum of Natural History in a dry and lonely part of Montana called Hell Creek. There he found the skeleton of an unknown dinosaur embedded in the hard sandstone of a hillside.

CANADA

MONTANA ⬦Hell Creek

NORTH DAKOTA

IDAHO

WYOMING

SOUTH DAKOTA

NEBRASKA

UTAH

COLORADO

KANSAS

Brown and the other fossil hunters were amazed by the dinosaur's enormous teeth. These six-inch daggers were sharp and sturdy, and both edges were serrated like steak knives. There was no doubt about it—they were made for eating meat. This was the largest carnivore anyone had ever seen. Henry Fairfield Osborn, a director at the museum, named it *Tyrannosaurus rex*—the "tyrant lizard king." Since that time, more than twenty *T. rex*es have been found in the ancient rocks of Wyoming, South Dakota, and Colorado, as well as Montana.

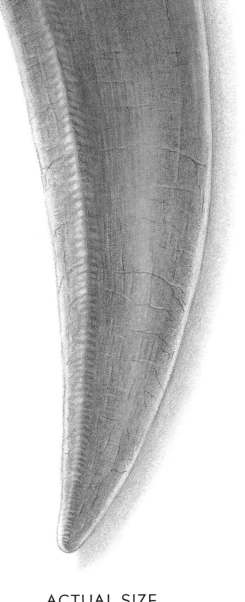

ACTUAL SIZE

Paleontologists
have worked for
many years removing
T. rex bones from rock
and joining them together
as they would have been in life.
From snout to tail, a *T. rex* was about forty
feet long and weighed more than six tons—about the length and
weight of a large truck. It stood fifteen feet high—tall enough
to peer into your second-floor bedroom window.

Judging by *T. rex*'s size, it must have needed to eat a *lot* of meat. But exactly what kinds of creatures did *T. rex* eat?

Seventy million years ago, when *T. rex* lived, America looked much different than it does today. Now herds of sheep and cattle browse the dry, short-grass prairies of the western states.

There were no sheep or cattle in *T. rex*'s time.
The weather was warmer and wetter than it is
today. And instead of dry prairie, much of the area
was lush woodland.

Plant-eating, or herbivorous, dinosaurs roamed the forests. They
did not munch grass, as sheep and cattle do—there was no grass in
dinosaur time.

They lived on ferns, berry bushes,
magnolias, ancient pines, and
sycamore trees.

When a *T. rex* was hungry, it had a choice of plant eaters to sink its teeth into:

Armored dinosaurs, such as *Euoplocephalus,* were common. These two-ton beasts were probably slow and plodding. But they were built like tanks, with hard bony plates to protect their heads, sharp studs on their backs, and sixty-pound clubs at the ends of their powerful tails.

Horned dinosaurs,
such as *Triceratops*, also
lived in *T. rex* country. These
were hulking creatures, weighing as
much as six tons. Their skulls are among
the largest of any animal that has ever
lived. Three fearsome, sharp horns
jutted forward from a *Triceratops*'s
snout and forehead.

Sauropods, such as the truly gigantic *Apatosaurus*, had nearly all died out by *T. rex*'s time. But one type—a pillar-legged, long-necked behemoth called *Alamosaurus*, still lived in the dryer areas. *Alamosaurus* was huge—up to seventy feet long and weighing twenty tons. Bigger than three *T. rex*es put together!

Duck-billed dinosaurs, such as *Edmontosaurus*, gathered in herds of thousands. Each grown duckbill was nearly the size of a *T. rex*. The adults in a herd may have kept watch for predators, such as *T. rex*, and bellowed a warning if one came near.

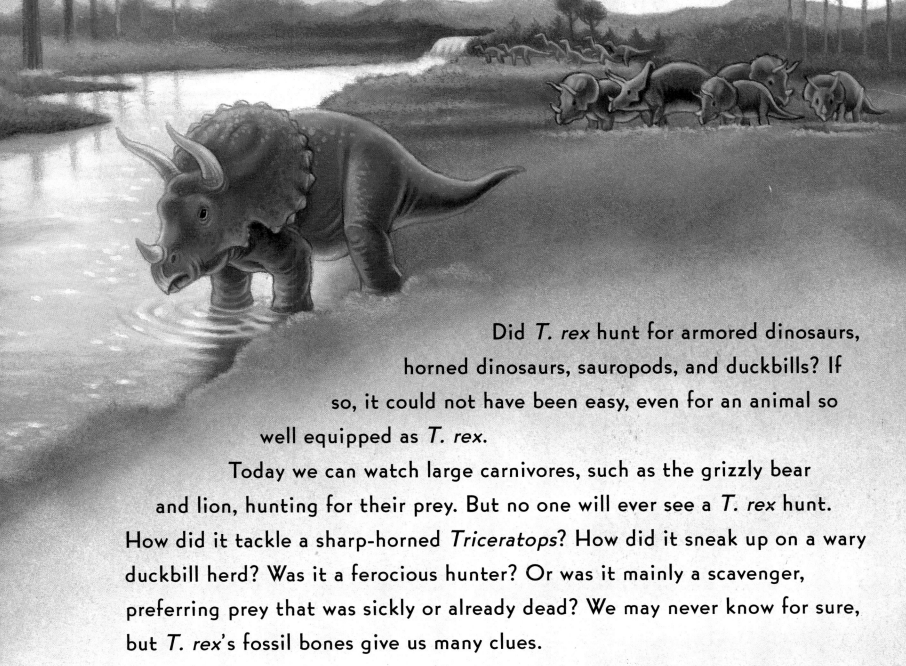

Did *T. rex* hunt for armored dinosaurs, horned dinosaurs, sauropods, and duckbills? If so, it could not have been easy, even for an animal so well equipped as *T. rex*.

Today we can watch large carnivores, such as the grizzly bear and lion, hunting for their prey. But no one will ever see a *T. rex* hunt. How did it tackle a sharp-horned *Triceratops*? How did it sneak up on a wary duckbill herd? Was it a ferocious hunter? Or was it mainly a scavenger, preferring prey that was sickly or already dead? We may never know for sure, but *T. rex*'s fossil bones give us many clues.

Fossils tell us that *T. rex* had a huge, toothy skull. Its jaws were powered by enormous muscles attached to a crest of bone on top of its skull and along its lower jaw. *T. rex*'s terrifying teeth and jaws were strong enough to rip off a hunk of meat the size of an entire cow in a single bite. If *T. rex* knocked out a few of its teeth on its armored prey, new teeth would grow to replace them.

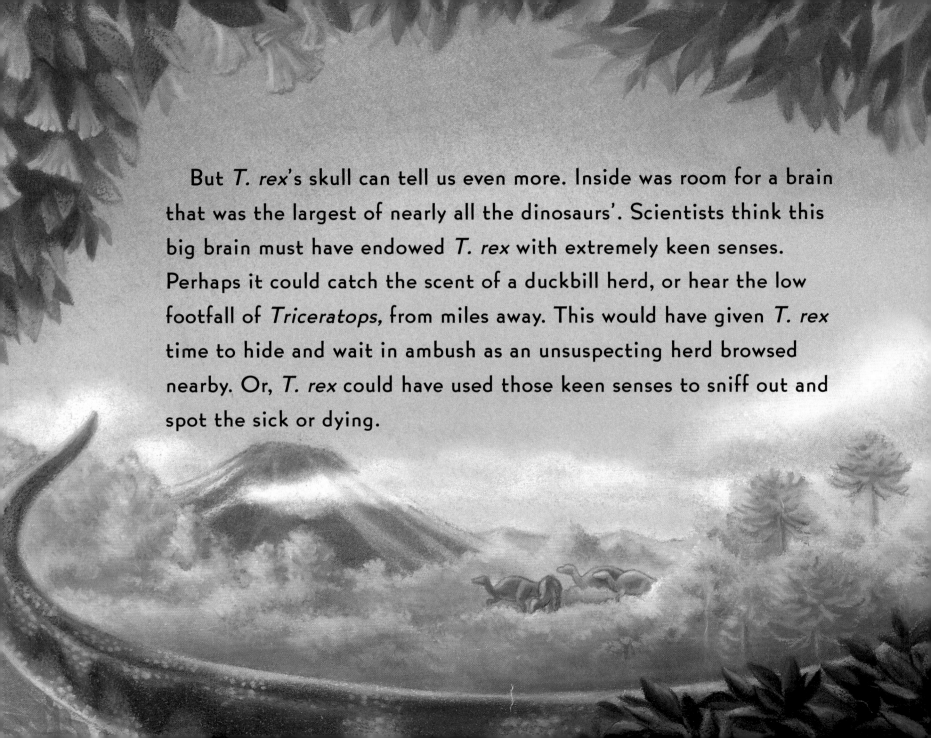

But *T. rex*'s skull can tell us even more. Inside was room for a brain that was the largest of nearly all the dinosaurs'. Scientists think this big brain must have endowed *T. rex* with extremely keen senses. Perhaps it could catch the scent of a duckbill herd, or hear the low footfall of *Triceratops*, from miles away. This would have given *T. rex* time to hide and wait in ambush as an unsuspecting herd browsed nearby. Or, *T. rex* could have used those keen senses to sniff out and spot the sick or dying.

Like other carnivores, *T. rex*'s eyes faced forward in its head. Today the greatest hunters, such as hawks and owls, lions and bears, have forward-facing eyes. This makes them good at judging how close or far away their prey is. Perhaps *T. rex* had eyes like a hawk's. With its strong, flexible, S-shaped neck, *T. rex* could swing its head around to look in all directions. It would have been hard for animals to hide from sharp-eyed *T. rex*. But once it found its prey, it would still have to catch and kill it.

One thing is certain: *T. rex* could not have used its arms to catch or kill. They were puny! Some scientists think *T. rex* may have used them to push itself up after it had fallen or lain down to rest. But were they big enough even for that? Those arms and small, two-clawed hands are a mystery.

T. rex's legs, however, were long and strong. And many scientists think *T. rex* must have been a good runner. Its bones were hollow, much like a bird's. The hollow bones would have kept *T. rex* from being too heavy and may have added to its speed.

Just how fast could *T. rex* run? No one knows for sure. The duckbills were probably the fastest herbivores *T. rex* ate. But duckbills did not have hollow bones. *T. rex* must have been at least as fast as a heavy duckbill, and probably faster.

The large claws on *T. rex*'s three-toed feet may have gripped the ground when it made quick turns in pursuit of prey. Once its prey was caught, *T. rex* could have held the animal down with those claws while it tore out bites with its teeth. Strong leg and neck muscles would have helped *T. rex* overpower a struggling giant.

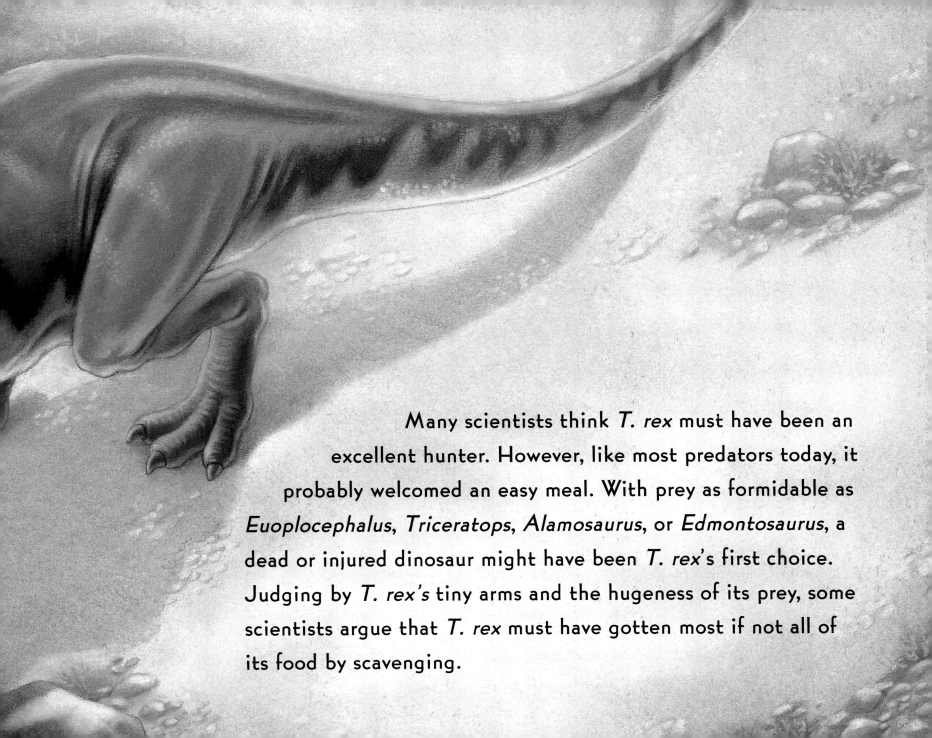

Many scientists think *T. rex* must have been an excellent hunter. However, like most predators today, it probably welcomed an easy meal. With prey as formidable as *Euoplocephalus*, *Triceratops*, *Alamosaurus*, or *Edmontosaurus*, a dead or injured dinosaur might have been *T. rex*'s first choice. Judging by *T. rex*'s tiny arms and the hugeness of its prey, some scientists argue that *T. rex* must have gotten most if not all of its food by scavenging.

There is much we do not know about the great *Tyrannosaurus rex*. Still, when we look at *T. rex*'s skeleton in the museum, it's fun to imagine what this creature might have been like in life, with his long stride, his head held down, teeth flashing.

Perhaps *T. rex* was the color of trees. He might have hidden quietly, awaiting his prey. When the moment was right, he would have sprung out in a quick burst of speed, his strong tail held straight out behind for balance. And then—*SNAP*—the most powerful jaws on earth would close. Even the huge *Alamosaurus* wouldn't stand a chance. In this world, *T. rex* was king.

FIND OUT MORE ABOUT T. REX RELATIVES

TYRANNOSAURUS REX is the most famous
member of the tyrannosaur, or tyrannosaurid,
family. The tyrannosaurids lived during the Cretaceous
Period (144 to 65 million years ago). Like *Tyrannosaurus rex,*
they all had large heads, sharp teeth, small forearms with two-clawed
hands, and long legs with three-toed feet.

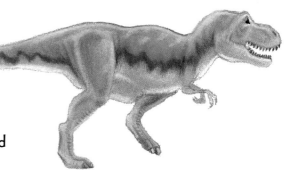

DASPLETOSAURUS—Smaller than *T. rex*—about twenty-
eight feet in length and weighing three tons. *Daspletosaurus*
lived before *T. rex* evolved, and some scientists think it may
have been a *T. rex* ancestor.

NANOTYRANNUS—The smallest of the tyrannosaurids, it
lived at the same time as *T. rex. Nanotyrannus* grew to "only"
about fifteen feet in length—less than half the size of *T. rex*—
and some scientists believe it was a young *T. rex* rather than a
different type of tyrannosaur.

ALBERTOSAURUS—A smaller cousin, who lived in North America at the same time as *T. rex*. *Albertosaurus* grew to be about twenty-six feet long and weighed as much as two tons.

TARBOSAURUS—A little lighter in build than *T. rex*, and smaller—up to thirty-three feet long. It was otherwise nearly identical to *T. rex*. *Tarbosaurus* terrorized plant eaters in Asia at about the same time *T. rex* lived in North America. Some scientists think the first North American *T. rex*es were *Tarbosaurus*es that migrated from Asia when the continents were linked by a bridge of land.

SIAMOTYRANNUS—"The tyrant from Thailand" may be the earliest known tyrannosaur. Bones from only its tail and hips have been found. Its exact size is not known.